→INTRODUCING

ALAIN BADIOU

MICHAEL J. KELLY & PIERO

Published in
the UK and the USA
in 2014 by Icon Books Ltd,
Omnibus Business Centre,
39–41 North Road, London N7 9DP
email: info@iconbooks.com
www.introducingbooks.com

Sold in the UK, Europe and Asia
by Faber & Faber Ltd,
Bloomsbury House,
74–77 Great Russell Street,
London WC1B 3DA or their agents

Distributed in South Africa
by Jonathan Ball,
Office B4, The District,
41 Sir Lowry Road,
Woodstock 7925

Distributed in Australia and
New Zealand
by Allen & Unwin Pty Ltd,
PO Box 8500,
83 Alexander Street,
Crows Nest, NSW 2065

Distributed to the trade in the USA
by Consortium Book Sales
and Distribution
The Keg House,
34 Thirteenth Avenue NE, Suite 101,
Minneapolis, MN 55413-1007

Distributed in Canada
by Penguin Books Canada,
90 Eglinton Avenue East,
Suite 700, Toronto,
Ontario M4P 2Y3

ISBN: 978-184831-665-2

Edited by Duncan Heath

Printed and bound in the UK by Clays Ltd, St Ives plc

Introducing Alain Badiou

French philosopher Alain Badiou has now been publishing for 50 years. His works range from novels, poems, "romanopéras" and popular political treatises to elaborate philosophical arguments engaging with mathematical theory.

Although the specific topics and characters differ between the texts, one can see throughout all of his writings, lectures and interviews an endless commitment to emancipatory politics and radical change through a fidelity to what he terms the **event** and its **truth**.

Badiou is most recognized internationally for his collection of three books on **subjectivity** (theories about the ways, or forms, in which a body enters into a relationship with reality, and truths) and the role of the event and truth in **ontology** (theory of being, in and of itself): *Theory of the Subject* (*Théorie du Sujet*, 1982), *Being and Event* (*L'Être et l'événement*, 1988) and *Logics of Worlds: Being and Event II* (*L'Être et l'événement Tome 2, Logiques des mondes*, 2006).

It was with the translation of *Being and Event* in 2005 that Badiou's fame spread into the English-speaking world, though it can be argued that *Theory of the Subject* is the most important work of the three.

Badiou in the world

In his short article "Philosophy as Biography", as a pun on Nietzsche's dictum that "philosophy is always a biography of the philosopher", Badiou suggests that his philosophy is his autobiography. This is in many ways quite clear.

A self-defined "provincial boy", Badiou was born on 17 January 1937 in Rabat, French-occupied Morocco, the son of a well-educated, upper-middle-class family. His mother attended the prestigious École Normale Supérieure (ENS) in Paris.

MY MOTHER STUDIED FRENCH LITERATURE. MY FATHER FOUGHT IN THE FRENCH RESISTANCE DURING THE SECOND WORLD WAR, AND LATER WAS THE SOCIALIST MAYOR OF TOULOUSE BEFORE BECOMING A PROFESSOR OF MATHEMATICS.

Following his parents, Badiou graduated from the ENS. Unlike their work in literature and mathematics, though, Badiou studied philosophy.

Some philosophers have criticized Badiou for supposedly jolting back and forth between maths and literature too easily; but regardless, it doesn't take a psychoanalyst to see the family's intellectual trinity wrapped up in the figure of Badiou, the embodied mediation between his parents.

The family connection to the École Normale Supérieure does not end for Badiou with his time as a student there. In 1999 he became chair of Philosophy at ENS, after 30 years teaching Philosophy at the University of Paris VIII (Vincennes-St Denis) and two years in Reims from 1966–7. Currently he is the René Descartes Chair at the European Graduate School, a small, private college on top of the Alps in the resort town of Saas-Fee, Switzerland.

The writing event

Badiou began his writing career in the early 1960s when he was affiliated with the "epistemology circle" (epistemology is the study of knowledge), a group of ENS students who published the journal *Les cahiers pour l'analyse*. It was in this journal that Badiou would publish some of his earliest philosophical texts. The first was called "Infinitesimal Subversion" in 1968, and a year later "Mark and Lack: On Zero".

In 1964 Badiou published his first book, *Almagestes*.

His first book of philosophy is *The Concept of Model* (*Le Concept de modèle*) published in 1969.

...n-Paul Sartre (1905–80) was essentially his total intellectual master during the whole of Badiou's early life as a philosopher, he tells us. The first theoretical text that sparked Badiou's interest in philosophy, and one relatively contemporary to him, was Sartre's *Sketch of a Theory of the Emotions* (1939).

With two committed Sartreans, Emmanuel Terry and Pierre Verstraeten, he also interrogated Sartre's *Critique of Dialectical Reason* (1960).

The seductiveness of philosophy

Badiou turned away from Sartre, but he remained confident in his desire to become a philosopher. The deeper reason is likely that his family situation and education led him to it, but there is another more tangible one too, perhaps.

THERE IS SOMETHING SEXUALLY SEDUCTIVE ABOUT BEING A PHILOSOPHER. WHY? SIMPLY SPEAKING, IT IS INTERESTING.

PHILOSOPHY PREPARES ONE TO BE UNIQUE, TO HAVE THE CONFIDENCE TO SPEAK, TO BE ABLE TO MAKE COMPLICATED ARGUMENTS AS OPPOSED TO SIMPLY PROPOSING TO A GIRL OR GUY.

What better reason can there be for becoming a philosopher, he jokingly asks. More seriously, he believes that the role of the philosopher is to challenge society simply because it is the way it is. To never give up. Finally, to always corrupt the youth!

Badiou's philosophy

Badiou's philosophy is a defence of **metaphysics** – the study of being in the world (as opposed to ontology, the examination of being in and of itself) – and also an expression of his politics.

MY PHILOSOPHY IS A LONG RESPONSE TO JACQUES DERRIDA, PHILIPPE LACOUE-LABARTHE, JEAN-LUC NANCY, AND JEAN-FRANÇOIS LYOTARD.

All these thinkers accept, following on from **Martin Heidegger** (1889–1976), the end of philosophy in its metaphysical form, and the elevating of places outside of philosophy as the appropriate spaces for serious thought, such as art, psychoanalysis, politics, etc.

AS A RESULT, PHILOSOPHY NO LONGER KNOWS ITS PROPER PLACE. IT IS LOST. IT EITHER FINDS FULFILMENT IN MAKING A MUSEUM OF ITSELF (I.E. HISTORY OF PHILOSOPHY), OR SEEKS TO FIND EXPRESSION THROUGH THESE ALTERNATIVE SITES.

Against this line of thinking Badiou claims that philosophy is not only possible today, but that it is **necessary**, that we should return to it in its classical sense, which means not only a strict separation between philosophy and all that is subject-dependent (reality, the world), but also the individual articulation of being (event), subject and truth.

Event, subject, truth

Badiou's philosophy thus revolves around three main ideas: the **event**, **subject** and **truth**, supplemented by a host of concepts including: situation, void, knowledges, world, and appearing. These will be covered at the appropriate points later on, but what is most imperative to keep in mind throughout is that philosophy is for Badiou a *way of thinking*, of seizing a truth.

Philosophy is an operation that of itself produces nothing; it operates on the basis of truths subtracted from the event.

The event, or, being and event

Badiou's most famous works of philosophy are without doubt his *Being and Event* and its sequel *Logics of Worlds: Being and Event II*. In these he claims that being is tied fundamentally to events, and that being-in-the-world – a body's relationship to the present – changes only upon the chance occurrence of an event **and** its announcement by subjects faithful to it.

What is the event, then?

THE EVENT (A REAL CHANGE, ONE THAT ACTUALLY ALTERS THE INTENSITY OF EXISTENCE) IS WHAT MAKES PHILOSOPHY POSSIBLE, AND NECESSARY.

14

The event is a condition for philosophy in that it brings into existence (through the subsequent eventual truth procedures, explained below) truths that are **prior-existent**, or **inexistent** (in the world but not active, i.e. latent truths), but that need an event to make them appear.

The event and its response

The event originates within a situation, not external to it, occurring at the site in which the possibility of an alternative truth exists, the point of **excess** within the situation, or in other words, with what cannot be brought into the ideological, linguistic norm of that world. An example would be those outside of capitalism today.

The event is then defined by its capacity to make this latent truth appear in the world, or as Badiou formulates it:

$$E\phi = 0$$

(Event x Inexistent = zero
[new existence])

In this formalization we see that the event is the moment at which existence begins.

IT IS BUT A FLEETING INSTANT LEAVING ONLY A TRACE OF ITSELF (THE **EVENT-TRACE**), YET IT HAS MADE APPEAR A NEW TRUTH THAT BY ITS VERY PRESENCE DEMANDS A RESPONSE.

This response by the subject, this subjective choice, can take one of three forms in relation to the event and the new truth that has emerged: acceptance, or, fidelity; denial/reaction against; or the occulting of the pre-evental situation (that is, the fetishizing of the previous status quo: "Things used to be so wonderful back when …").

The subject

Okay, so what exactly is the subject?

THE SUBJECT REPRESENTS NOT THE INDIVIDUAL, BUT WHAT THE INDIVIDUAL IS ULTIMATELY CAPABLE OF BECOMING.

For Badiou, the subject is a mode by which "a body enters into a subjective formalism with regard to the production of a present". Subjective formalism is the form chosen for the body's relationship to the present (particularly in light of the event and new truth).

A subject is born not simply from the event – which brings forth truth via one of four conditions (explained below) – but is dependent on its own affective conditions that include its relationship not only to the event and new truth but to a **body**.

This body is what will determine the path, procedure, existence, and presentation into a new reality of a truth according to the form the subject takes. There are, as mentioned above, three possible subjective forms for Badiou: the **faithful**, the **reactionary** and the **obscure**.

Badiou's theory of the subject demands that the general field of subjectivity (see diagram, p. 32) is initiated by the faithful subject, who makes evident the existence of a particular situation, a present.

THIS FAITHFUL SUBJECT IS THE ONE THAT PROCLAIMS: "YES, AN EVENT HAS INDEED HAPPENED, AND IT HAS BROUGHT A NEW TRUTH INTO EXISTENCE!"

As such, the faithful subject creates a general subjective situation in which all bodies in that world **must** make a choice on what type of subject they will be – faithful, reactionary or obscure – in relation to the present, given the proclamation by the faithful of an event and new truth. The inaugurator of the general subjective field is thus the faithful subject.

From this point – the realization of the alternative truth – forward, the reactive and obscure subjects are there as rivals. The reactionary subject works to weaken the fabric of the new, while the obscure subject occults the appearance of the situation.

ONCE THE SUBJECTIVE PROCESS BEGINS, ONCE AN EVENT HAPPENS AND A NOVEL TRUTH APPEARS, ALL THREE SUBJECTIVE FORMS WILL EMERGE!

The mathemes

Below are the mathemes Badiou constructs to represent these subjects, along with further explanation:

Faithful subject

Matheme:

OR

The body divided by many points (confronted by the totality of the existing world and needing to make a decision, ¢) is subordinated to the trace event (ε), the consequence of which is the production of a new reality (π), the emancipated present. Fidelity means the transition from random encounter with truth to a more permanent constitution.

Reactive subject

Matheme:

OR

The would-be faithful subject (the total matheme above) is subordinated by the negation of the trace event (¬ε), the consequence being the denial of a new reality (π̄).

We can see in this formula that reaction preserves – in its articulated unconscious – the form of the faithful subject. It does not seek to eliminate the present, even the new reality, but simply maintain that the eventual, faithful break is useless. Such a subject is represented by those afraid of the event, of radically tearing apart the present through a **militant fidelity to a truth.**

EXAMPLES OF REACTIONARY SUBJECTS ARE: RADICAL ARTISTS RECYCLED INTO THE ACADEMIC WORLD, OLD SCIENTISTS UNAWARE OF INNOVATIVE MOVEMENTS IN THEIR FIELD, RENEGADES OR THERMIDORIANS (TRAITORS TO THE EVENT, APOSTATES TO THE NEW TRUTH), OR LOVERS TRAPPED BY ROUTINE.

The analogy of love

Concerning the last two examples, fidelity to a truth is often expressed by Badiou in terms analogous to the common notion of faithfulness in love.

These would-be lovers promote and enjoy not the trust in differences like in love but in the anxieties and suspicions about difference; identity is at the heart of all reaction. For Badiou it is the apostate Thermidorian that is the most dangerous of all. This is the reactive subject that is initially faithful to the truth and creation of an alternative situation, but reacts against it, abandons the fight. This sense of political abandonment is very real to Badiou, as we'll see later in the discussion of May 1968 in Paris.

Finally, the matheme for the **obscure subject.**

Matheme:

OR

The obscure subject tries to fulfil the abolished present (π) with a dogma, an atemporal filling by a monstrous, totalized body such as a God, race, city, etc. The obscure subject radically resists the new truth, rejects change, demands hatred of pure thoughts, promises salvation through an absolute body (C), as opposed to through a(n absolute) truth.

Chance and the subject

Chance is a central feature of Badiou's philosophy of the subject.
The subject is the result of the unexpected chance of the event and the
performance of chance at the point of subjective qualification
(when the subjective position is determined).

Although the event – an excess of existence breaking into being – needs
certain philosophical conditions, the emergence of the subject is
nevertheless the result of the chance occurrence of the event.

This axiom holds for all of Badiou's truth procedures: they need a chance initiation. This is not a passive chance, the chance of doing nothing, of non-thinking, which is that of the non-subject – the objective (epistemological) status quo – it is an active thinking, one that takes the chance to break wholly from one's world, one's existing reality. This is evident in all of Badiou's discussions on science, art, love and politics.

> WE MUST BE WILLING TO ABANDON (TEAR OUR BODIES AWAY FROM) OUR SITUATIONS AND WORLDS AS THEY ARE IN ORDER TO BE FAITHFUL TO THE NEW EVENT OF LOVE, POLITICS, ART OR SCIENCE.

This is the choice that qualifies the subject as faithful, reactive or obscure, and ultimately as either ethical or unethical (as we will see below).

Truth(s)

What is a truth? The insistence on the need for the category of truth in philosophy (via Plato) is a central feature of Badiou's philosophy, and part of his unique place today against the broader stream of **sophistic** or **postmodernist** thought. In his understanding of what truth is, its ontological site and its role in philosophy, we can clearly see everything that Badiou represents as a thinker, both philosophically and politically.

In 1960, when Badiou was still a young man, he met with a group of striking Belgian mineworkers. This experience had a profound impact on him, to the extent that in retrospect it was a key occasion in cementing his commitment to emancipatory politics.

AFTER THIS FORMATIVE MOMENT I GAVE MYSELF THE TASK OF TRANSFORMING THE CONCEPT OF TRUTH TO EQUATE WITH EGALITARIANISM.

To do so, Badiou gave to truth three basic attributes:

1. TRUTH DEPENDS ON RUPTURE AND EVENT, NOT ON STRUCTURE.
2. TRUTH IS UNIVERSAL, AND GENERAL (HAS GENERICITY).
3. TRUTH CONSTITUTES ITS SUBJECT (I.E. ITS APPEARANCE VIA THE EVENT DEMANDS A SUBJECTIVE RESPONSE, ITS "MILITANT ATTRIBUTE").

Thus, as suggested above, a *truth emerges only through the appearing of an event*; it is the appearing of a prior-inexistent within a situation of bodies and languages. A truth does not emerge immediately from the event, as the event only opens up the **possibility** of a truth.

A truth comes to being during the subjective process, the appearing (or small 'l' logic) of a subject (when the faithful subject proclaims it), during the subject's decision of fidelity, reaction or occultation (obscuring) of an event and its trace.

Together this demonstrates Badiou's materialism (truth emerges from a real existence) and explains his general maxim:

THERE ARE ONLY BODIES AND LANGUAGES, EXCEPT THAT THERE ARE TRUTHS.

In the second and third attributes Badiou is arguing that a *subject cannot constitute a truth* (only respond to it), thereby confirming the earlier point that truth is general and universal – it is not tied to any specific, historical, subject – and so able to be re-actualized *ad infinitum*.

The trajectory of a truth

All being is multiple for Badiou, represented by epistemological sets, subsets of knowledge within the world. Truths proceed within such sets, within what Badiou terms a "situation", that is, a generic multiplicity of knowledge/language, circumstances and objects.

TRUTH (LIKE THE EVENT) IS MATERIALLY DERIVED; IT IS NEVER TRANSCENDENTAL IN THE SENSE OF CREATED FROM OUTSIDE OF BEING.

IT FORMS AND FESTERS AS AN INEXISTENT WITHIN A SITUATION UNTIL THE CHANCE OCCURRENCE OF THE EVENT MAKES IT APPEAR.

Truths thus are the result of, can only be the truth of, the material situation of being, material existence.

The situation reflects a multitude of subsets, the collection of which Badiou terms **knowledges.** A truth is distinguished from a knowledge via the void …

THAT IS, A TRUTH IS A POINT OF THINKING, A RUPTURE TO KNOWLEDGE (BROUGHT BY THE ANNOUNCEMENT OF THE TRUTH-EVENT BY THE FAITHFUL SUBJECT), A HOLE OR VOID IN KNOWING, A SITE OF THINKING.

This is the power of the truth, and of the anti-philosopher whose role is to think this void (the philosopher interrogates the new truth that emerges – the anti-philosopher and philosopher thus complementing each other), to in a sense negate but more appropriately to **subtract** (the inexistent) from the status quo of knowing.

31

The gamma diagram

The gamma diagram of the trajectory of a truth represents this process of subtraction, of subtracting a truth from the situation, an inexistent from the existent. It is extremely important to Badiou's philosophy since it represents his formal conception of truth. Its features will be looked at in more detail on pages 34 to 41.

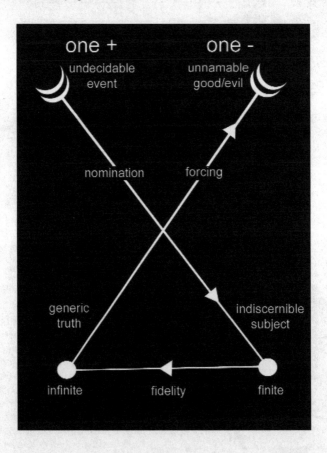

A truth does not immediately materialize from the event; it comes into being through a process that is begun by the event.

There are four possible truth processes, or rather "truth procedures", through which a truth can come into being. In no definite order, the truth procedures are: **art**, **love**, **maths/science** and **politics**.

THESE CONDITIONS FOR TRUTH REPRESENT THE ONLY FOUR PLACES FROM WHICH A NEW TRUTH CAN MATERIALIZE AND THE PROCESS OF SUBTRACTION BEGIN.

THEY ARE THE ABSOLUTE **CONDITIONS FOR PHILOSOPHY** SINCE WITHOUT THEM THERE IS NO TRIAD OF BEING, SUBJECT AND TRUTH.

The subtractive process

So, let's go through the details of the subtractive process, the trajectory of a truth, from its emergence to its closure. The coming into being of a truth through one of the four procedures is determined by four modalities: the undecidable, the indiscernible, the generic and the unnameable.

The path of the nascent truth begins first and foremost with the event. The event brings into view the **undecidable**, something unknown to the existing world (so, the prior-inexistent).

ONCE THIS OCCURS, THE EVENT AND THE TRUTH THAT APPEARS GO THROUGH A PROCESS OF **NOMINATION** WHEN A BODY AND LANGUAGE ATTEMPT TO GIVE A NAME TO THE EVENT AND ITS NEW TRUTH.

The **indiscernible** is the point at which the subject is founded. It is the moment when an attempt must be made to reconcile the event and new truth with existing knowledge, existing language. The indiscernible is when the subject actually splits from the plane of reality in the process of subjectivation. It is the subtractive point at which the choice is made about a body's relation to the event and new truth.

In the first two modalities the truth emerges from the void, the split in knowledge, from the infinity of the undecidable, the moment of the event, to the finite point of indiscernibility when the subject is born (when choices are made).

COMMUNAL EXISTENCE

IT IS IN THE TIME BETWEEN THE SECOND AND THIRD MODALITIES, THE INDISCERNIBLE AND THE GENERIC, THAT A TRUTH IS FORMALLY SUBJECTED.

What is the generic?

COMMUNAL EXISTENCE

THE GENERIC MODALITY REPRESENTS THE FULL GLORY AND POWER OF TRUTH IN THE WORLD.

AFTER A DECISION IS MADE AROUND THE MOMENT OF THE INDISCERNIBLE MODALITY TO BE FAITHFUL TO THIS NEW TRUTH, THE FAITHFUL SUBJECT HAS EMERGED.

The faithful subject in this act confirms the event and tries to create meaning for the new truth via this faithfulness to the trace of the event.

Thus the generic modality is what is reached through the subject's recognizing the truth as not part of the existing situation, and the subsequent *pure point* of decision to be faithful to it.

IT IS THE PRODUCTION OF A NEW PRESENT BY THE FORMAL SUBJECT TYPE **FAITHFUL**, AS BORNE BY A BODY.

Forcing

Since truth is infinite and generic, the way to the final modality, the unnameable, can only be represented by the future perfect. This is the act of **forcing**, of forcing a future history for the truth.

> THOSE FAITHFUL TO A REVOLUTION WILL ANNOUNCE THAT THE FUTURE WILL BE DIFFERENT! AND MOREOVER, THAT WE KNOW THE PATH OF THE FUTURE: IT IS THROUGH THIS NEW TRUTH, FIDELITY TO THE EVENT, WHICH WILL DETERMINE OUR PATH TOWARDS EMANCIPATION.

Therefore, forcing is what authorizes the anticipation of knowledge, about what will have been if a truth could reach completion. It is the pre-emptive attempt to determine the truth.

The unnameable

Once the infinite truth of a generic subset of universality is forced via the future perfect, we reach in the subtractive process the final ontological stage in the truth procedure: the **unnameable**.

Forcing creates the false impression that the truth continues from the generic upon a path to completion.

The unnameable is not in itself unnameable in terms of lack of knowledge/language, but because it is out of reach to the anticipations that are founded on the truth.

Out of desire for the particular, finite manifestation of the truth that occurred during the act of forcing, that is, towards love of the unnameable, this excess will displace the power of the truth – in its infinite, generic form – from appearance. And so we start again.

The return of Plato

Badiou is a neo-Platonist. He believes that **Friedrich Nietzsche** (1844–1900) was correct to suggest that Europe would from his time try to cure itself of the "Plato disease", that what **Plato** (c. 428–348 BC) had initiated historically was entering into the closing of its effect …

PLATO'S REIGN IS OVER!

BUT NOW PLATO IS BACK … AND SO ARE UNIVERSAL TRUTHS (DOWN WITH THE SOPHISTS)!

The conditions for philosophy

Badiou returns us to Plato by focusing on three key notions in Plato's work:

1. Attentiveness to the conditions of philosophy and the necessity of philosophy's dialogue with art and poetry, mathematics, love and politics. In other words, Badiou is faithful to the role Plato gives to "conditions" for philosophy, and the conditions under which philosophy can be.

2. Philosophy is nothing without the category of Truth. Although it opens him up to criticism for being "anti-contemporary", Badiou firmly argues that philosophy has little meaning without the idea that there can be and are eternal truths …

AGAINST THE ARGUMENTS OF THE MODERN SOPHISTS LIKE JEAN-FRANÇOIS LYOTARD, TRUTH IS A CENTRAL, NECESSARY CATEGORY OF PHILOSOPHY.

3. Plato has been misunderstood. Instead of being concerned with the transcendence of ideas, what he really cares about is the question, "What is thinking?"

In the dialogues, especially the later ones, such as the *Sophist*, the *Parmenides* and the *Philebus*, Plato poses the question, "What is thought?" in order to ask:

WHAT IS AN INTERNAL ARTICULATION BETWEEN IDEAS, WHAT IS THE MOVEMENT OF THOUGHT, WHAT IS ITS INTERNAL ALTERITY, ITS IMPASSE, AND SO ON? FOR ME, THIS IS PLATO.

The four truth procedures

Badiou's philosophy depends upon what he calls the four truth procedures, or generic conditions for philosophy. These are the conditions under which a truth can emerge from an event (an event can occur only under these four conditions), and hence the subject can come into being and the subjective process can travel through its possibilities of becoming.

The four conditions are:

Art
(the plastic arts, music, poetry, literature, theatre, dance and cinema)

Love
(emancipatory, amorous)

Science
(maths and physics)

Politics

By going through the truth procedures we can not only grasp a more tangible image of Badiou's overall ontology, from event to truth and subject, but we can also see how truth is absolute and its condition **immanent** (inherent).

Two key points about the function of conditions for truth must be kept in mind:

1. A truth can emerge only from one of these four conditions, and hence never from philosophy.

2. Truths are absolute. A truth is produced under, and testified by, only one of the conditions and belongs absolutely to it. Its procedure is immanent because it exposes an infinite truth to the finite.

The four conditions are not only fundamental for understanding Badiou's theory of being, but they form the bases of all of his writings. In fact, it is fair to suggest that his writings, lectures and interviews represent various applications and expressions of the possibilities for the event and for truth under one of the conditions of philosophy, that is to say *they are attempts to circumstance* his thought. We'll go through some of these circumstances in a bit, but first let's get a closer glimpse of the specific conditions.

Art

In the words of KRS-One, the hip-hop artist, political thinker and author of the *Gospel of Hip-Hop* (2009): "reality is not the truth, poetry is real life" (from his song "Reality"). And so it is with Badiou.

ART IS THAT WHICH ON THE LEVEL OF THOUGHT DOES FULL JUSTICE TO THE EVENT; IT IS THE REFLECTION ON THE EVENT AS SUCH.

What Badiou means is that art, out of all the truth procedures, exposes us most evidently to the realization that we live not only in a situation of ideology, but of truths. The true artistic event, one that ushers in a truth, is one that demonstrates to us that we speak and live among the inexistent and existent presence of the idea, the universal truth of which we must at certain times partake.

The example of the horses

Badiou provides two sets of complementary examples for this in art, both of which involve the depiction of horses.

The first set contains two cave paintings from different artists, drawn roughly 30,000 years ago and rediscovered in 1994, on walls in the Chauvet-Pont-d'Arc cave in the Ardèche region of France. In one of these a horse is drawn in a frame with white lines, while the other is a panel of four horses drawn in shades of grey and with remarkable clarity.

The other set of paintings comprises two works of Pablo Picasso: his "Two Horses Dragging a Slaughtered Horse" (1929) and "Man Holding Two Horses" (1939).

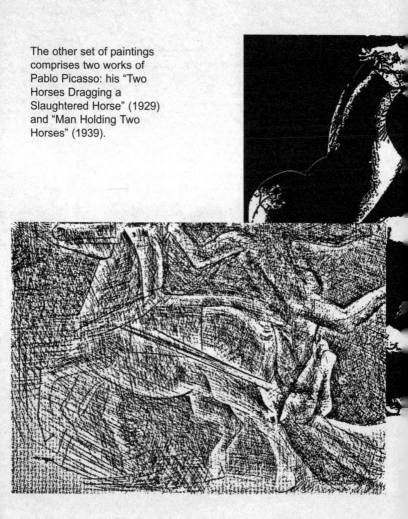

In the cave paintings, Badiou tell us, the artists are trying to capture on the wall not only the conquered savageness of the horses but awe over the beauty admired and dominated. In these expressions of painting-thought (the work of artistic truth production) the distance between painted and painter was not so far, there was a commonality with and praise of the horses. Picasso on the other hand saw in the horses the image of a declining peasant life, a rural innocence lost.

IN THESE PAINTINGS WE SEE A NOSTALGIA AND VANITY FOR THE HORSES.

Despite the very real differences and intentions in the existing worlds of the artists and the paintings, an eternal, artistically produced truth "horse" is evident in both.

In viewing them we can see that the theme of "horse" is **subtracted** from variation (variation of horse depictions, from 30,000 years ago to Picasso). This is why despite them existing in distant worlds, we are impressed by their beauty, of the idea of horse expressed.

Regardless of the uniqueness of the worlds of the cave painters, Picasso's and ours, animals are stable components of all of them, and this of course includes horses. The empirical experience with and of horses is different, but this is subordinated, Badiou says, to the stability of the idea, the truth "horse".

TO PAINT THE HORSE IS TO ASCEND TOWARDS THE IDEA; IT IS A MATERIALLY CREATED SENSIBILITY OF THE IDEA.

The artist declares this to be a horse, a truth at the point of the indiscernible … it is, following Plato's line of thinking, "horse" or "horseness" and not horses that we see.

Thus the horses of the Chauvet-Pont-d'Arc cave and of Picasso are representations of a universal truth. Appearing in radically different worlds, for disparate reasons, the horses as animal in each case are a demonstration of an artistic truth made by a subject, in that the animal as type is clear, in what Badiou calls "the formless continuity of sensorial experience".

WHAT THE MASTER OF THE CAVE PAINTING INITIATED (THOUGH S/HE MAY ALSO HAVE HAD A MASTER, AD INFINITUM) AND WHAT PICASSO REMINDS US WITH THE HORSE IS THAT BEING EXISTS NOT ONLY AMONG BODIES AND LANGUAGES, BUT AMONG TRUTHS.

Inaesthetics: defence of art as truth procedure

In his 1998 *Handbook of Inaesthetics (Petit manuel d'inesthetique)* Badiou presents his concept of "inaesthetics", built largely from the poetry of **Stéphane Mallarmé** (1842–98) and **Fernando Pessoa** (1888–1935) and the prose of **Samuel Beckett** (1906–89). He takes the reader through the question of the essence of a poem and of the relationship between art, poetry, aesthetics and his own idea of truth and the philosophy of the event.

Badiou repeats his argument that art is one of the four truth procedures, and that art is both immanent and singular.

IT IS **SINGULAR** IN THAT IT IS THE PRODUCER OF ITS OWN TRUTHS, WHICH ARE UNABLE TO BE REDUCED EITHER TO THE OTHER TRUTH PROCEDURES OR TO PHILOSOPHY.

Inaesthetics is a defence of this philosophical position. By it Badiou means to advance art as a producer of its own truths, and simultaneously argue against and prevent the turning of art into a philosophical object (aesthetics). Inaesthetics denies the relationship between the object and its reflection; it is opposed to looking at the aesthetics of art, its external effects, as object for inquiry, for philosophy.

Instead, art is a thought in which artworks are the truth and not the effect.

Inaesthetics serves as further support of Badiou's philosophical position. It is a case study in the truth procedure art, a long defence of the immanence and singularity of art and art's procedure …

The purpose of this text and the line of thinking of this argument is to use select poetry and prose to defend his philosophy of the event, his ontological structure of the subject.

A brief interlude: Samuel Beckett

Badiou's closest philosophical companion out of all 20th-century writers has been Samuel Beckett. Why?

BECKETT SHARPENED MY THINKING ON THE IDEA OF THE NOTION OF GENERIC TRUTH, OF THE GENERAL DISPOSAL OF ALL THE PRE-EXISTING FOUNDATIONS AND AGENCIES OF KNOWLEDGE IN THE BECOMING, THE ACTUALIZING, OF THE TRUE.

Okay, but why is Beckett interrupting us here? It is not only because Badiou credits Beckett for being able to clarify the idea of the genericity of truth. For Badiou, Beckett is also a figure who is himself almost generic and at the very least one whose works produce and discuss truths under at least two truth procedures (which is not to say across conditions): art and love.

In the artistic realm, where Beckett creates truth, it is through a reading of the beginning and ending of Beckett's novella, *Ill Seen Ill Said* (*Mal vu Mal dit*, 1981) by which Badiou concludes that the generic in art is precisely, as we see in the book, the move away from the adversity of life and its aesthetic to the happiness of the vision of the void, the excess of that situation, the truth that appears through the artistic event.

Love is, to no surprise, a common topic in art and popular culture, whether in poetry, literature, drama, cinema, music or any other artistic movement. Much of what is produced about love in art, Badiou contends, concerns the overcoming of obstacles to find love; this is the main theme.

Beckett is, for Badiou, unique in that contrary to this situation he is a writer concerned about the "obstinacy" of love.

We can see in Beckett's two-act play, *Happy Days*, a strange sort of fidelity to the event of love between the domineering wife Winnie and submissive husband Willie …

And Beckett's short work, *Enough*, is about an old couple still in love, about the endurance of life despite the slow and definite diminishing of the bodies and their sexualities, but again it encourages and embraces fidelity to the love event.

Thus we can see in Beckett not only the defence of the event and genericity of truth, but the importance of *fidelity to a truth*, a thesis central to Badiou's philosophy and politics. Now, on to love as truth procedure.

Love

LOVE, THE ESSENCE OF WHICH IS FIDELITY IN THE MEANING I GIVE TO THIS WORD, DEMONSTRATES HOW ETERNITY CAN EXIST WITHIN THE TIME SPAN OF LIFE ITSELF. HAPPINESS, IN A WORD! YES, HAPPINESS IN LOVE IS THE PROOF THAT TIME CAN ACCOMMODATE ETERNITY. AND YOU CAN ALSO FIND PROOF IN THE POLITICAL ENTHUSIASM YOU FEEL WHEN PARTICIPATING IN A REVOLUTIONARY ACT, IN THE PLEASURE GIVEN BY WORKS OF ART AND THE ALMOST SUPERNATURAL JOY YOU EXPERIENCE WHEN YOU AT LAST GRASP IN DEPTH THE MEANING OF A SCIENTIFIC THEORY.

BADIOU

Love is a truth procedure whose truths are separate from those of any of the others, but its truth and its event are possibly the easiest to generalize and from there to see the politics inherent in Badiou's philosophy. As such, love is possibly the most important of the truth procedures, next to politics, to Badiou's overall philosophical project.

I LIKE TO REPEAT THE MAXIM ATTRIBUTED TO PLATO: IF ONE'S STARTING-POINT OF INQUIRY IS NOT LOVE, THEN ONE WILL NEVER UNDERSTAND THE ESSENCE OF PHILOSOPHY.

Love begins, Badiou states, when something impossible is overcome; it is the breaking through of the event, as are the other truth procedures. There is, though, something more profoundly urgent, violent and impressive about the love event.

LOVE ERUPTS INTO ONE'S LIFE AND COMPLETELY SHATTERS THE SITUATION, THE ENTIRE PRESENT AND THE FUTURE OF THAT LIFE!

The philosophical and political importance of love then is clear; it has the power to change everything. Fidelity to it represents our ability to think differently, to make a radical decision to the alternative.

Love and the infinite

Love should not happen, since it is unexplainable according to the knowledge of the pre-existing situation, but it does, and when it does it demands a choice that means one can never return to the situation of before (once a truth has emerged the old situation can never be maintained).

LOVE IS FOR EVER. EVEN IF A COUPLE BREAKS UP, IF THEIR UNION WAS A TRUE LOVE EVENT THEN THAT LOVE IS INFINITE, REPRESENTING THE UNIVERSAL, GENERIC TRUTH OF LOVE (AND PROVIDING THE LOVERS WITH THE FEELING THAT FINITUDE, THEIR LIVES, CAN HANDLE THE INFINITE).

That love still exists even if it is latent, non-apparent, not in the situation of one's world, or inexistent.

This is Badiou's point about *all truths*. They inexist and can return at any time. Even if after the event of love we make poor decisions that lead to the failure/impossibility of fidelity to that event, to the extent that we break up and end the coupleship, that love, that truth, still exists.

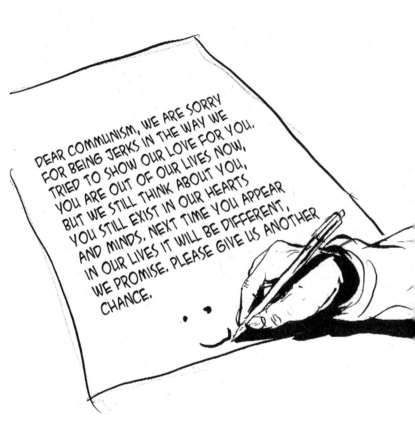

We can and should try to bring a love truth back into the world. To do so we go back to the point at which we made the bad decisions and try to make new ones, not to return to a situation, which is impossible, but to maintain fidelity to a truth. We should not to be afraid to fail again, even if it means more pain and suffering. We should embrace the feeling, the insatiable burning between the ribs, in the words of the 12th/13th-century Spanish-Arab poet Muhyiddin Ibn al-'Arabi.

In short, as Badiou succinctly declares:

What is love?

For the pop singer Haddaway, in his 1994 hit "What is Love?", love is tantamount simply to not being hurt and as such it is a perfect mainstream counterpoint to Badiou's theory of love, which could not be more opposite. For Haddaway, love means maintaining the status quo of a relationship above all else, without any regard to whether or not it is a true love event, without any restating of the love event.

Love without risk

Badiou attacks such a view of love as unquestioned stability in *In Praise of Love (Éloge de l'amour,* 2009) when he discusses the advertising slogans and sales promises made by a Parisian dating website.

THIS SITE, REPRESENTATIVE OF THE BROADER MOVEMENT IN DATING WEBSITES, PROMISES LOVE WITHOUT RISK, WITHOUT HAVING TO "FALL IN LOVE", TO HAVE LOVE WITHOUT THE CHANCE OF SUFFERING.

The website also promises to coach people in love. This type of dating, this service, this way of thinking love is what Badiou refers to as a "safety-first" concept of love.

This is a love that is secured against risks, it is the application of the business principles of risk management to love, selling you the confidence that you can have love only after fully assessing all of the inherent risks of the idea in general and the partner in particular and having made the conclusion that this is a risk-free partner for love. Reading Badiou's description of this strange and ethically perverse notion of love, one can feel and see the noxiousness and Badiou's disgust for it.

THIS SAFETY-FIRST, SUPPOSED RISK-FREE TYPE OF LOVE IS A REAL THREAT TO SOCIETY AND IS ANALOGOUS TO AN ARRANGED MARRIAGE, A MARRIAGE AGREED TO FOR THE SECURITY OF THE INDIVIDUAL (AND/OR [FUTURE] FAMILY).

To hell with others

The first threat then that this concept of love presents is that it turns love into a risk-enterprise, or rather, a matter of security. The second threat is that it creates a society in which people believe that risks are those of other people, and that if there does in fact arise any sort of problem in the relationship of love, then the appropriate, immediate response is to leave the person, ignoring their feelings, to prevent any further otherness from becoming actualized.

This narcissistic way of thinking Badiou likens to our modern politics: so long as we have the better armies, bombs, police, and more wealth, to hell with the other side, who are not part of our world.

For Badiou, we must, agreeing with the poet **Arthur Rimbaud** (1854–91), reinvent love, reinvent adventure, and risk security and ease, or "health and safety" as the British are fond of saying. In the words of a May 1968 slogan:

In the capitalist world we live in, it is generally believed that individuals pursue first and foremost their own self-interest.

This is why love, although a personal experience, has universal implications and is thus central to philosophy, as Plato was well aware and the first, Badiou says, to claim.

Love and the Christ event

We can see too in this argument a sort of sublimated Christianity: one must suffer for truth, for love, in order to know and be with the loved one. Christ makes the similar demand that to be with Him, to be with God, we must appreciate the suffering that love requires.

Badiou and Tupac

Let us turn to one of the most articulate and intellectual artists of our time, **Tupac Shakur** (1971–96), whose very name itself, let alone his words and the political and artistic truths he created, is the embodiment of radical, emancipatory thinking. It is with Tupac's thoughts on love that we find the closest relationship in perhaps all of contemporary music to Badiou's concept of love.

Tupac's song "Do for Love" opens with a slow, rhythmic verse in which he says he should have known that his lover was trouble right from the start, thus announcing love as the confrontation between the existing in the situation and the possibility of a new truth.

This is a traumatic encounter with a formerly inexistent that one knows is world-altering and as such is dangerous and risky, but has happened and cannot be avoided. A subjective decision must be made, and Tupac embraces the path of fidelity to love despite the very real chance of failure, the risks of pain.

Love versus desire

It is essential too that for Badiou love not be equated with desire, which unlike love is attention to a particular aspect of the other, such as buttocks, vagina, eyes, hair or cock, whereas love is a peering into and connection with the being of the other.

To those who say that this is overly romantic and/or that love does not exist – all that exists is desire and so go ahead and have sex, don't bother thinking or caring about the person, all that is real anyhow is sexual desire – Badiou says:

For Badiou, all that really exists is love, and desire is in fact the veneer. There is no such possibility as a "friend with benefits" or having sex with a friend. Friends simply do not have sex with each other.

Political truths

Politics as a truth procedure holds the same structure as the other conditions of art, science and love. It is, however, the one that attracts the majority of Badiou's attention.

The **circumstancing** of his politics (the application of the theory of the truth procedures into real-life politics) will be covered later, but here in the discussion of politics as **condition** it is imperative to grasp two aspects of the political truth.

FIRST, FOREMOST AND PERHAPS CONTRARY TO POPULAR BELIEF ABOUT THE TOPIC, POLITICS IS NOT THE SITE OF POWER.

POLITICS IS STRICTLY A REALM OF THOUGHT.

The purpose of politics is not change or conversion. Its singular aim, like that of the other truth procedures, is the invention of possibilities that could not hitherto be seen or considered.

Secondly, Badiou declares that philosophy has no meaning at all if it is not somehow connected to politics. What this means is that the political truth, of course immanent and absolute only within and to the realm of politics, must be a thought that is properly and fully considered once it comes into being through the political truth procedure.

THE ROLE OF THE PHILOSOPHER IS TO **INTERPRET** (NOT CREATE) TRUTHS, AND THE POLITICAL TRUTHS ARE THE MOST DIRECTLY PRESSING IN LIFE.

In this Badiou confirms his old Sartrean commitment to politics while maintaining a strict separation between philosophy and politics.

Politics is a thought, not a power of adaptation or transformation. A new political truth and radical political event are the result of the emergence of the *excess of the situation* (the actualizing of an inexistent). They are not the consequence of a pre-existing political relationship (e.g. of the masses, the French, the left, etc.) nor the effect of political action (e.g. democracy, voting, or all that is within the accepted state system).

POLITICAL TRUTH IS NOT THE CREATION OF A NEW SET OF ACCEPTABLE IDENTITIES BUT THE CREATION OF THE GENERIC EQUALITY THAT I CALL COMMUNISM.

It is the act of the impossible, realizing the prior-inexistent and thus the coming into being of the infinite.

Scientific/mathematical truths

A scientific event is one in which a universal truth of the mathematical or scientific kind is presented into a situation. From there it follows the truth procedure as already established.

The procedure of a mathematical truth may sound simple enough: that a mathematical idea is introduced into the world by, say, a mathematician.

The example of prime numbers

Early in *Logics of Worlds* Badiou presents the example of prime numbers as universal truths, and as such inexistent truths, or figures, waiting to be actualized. The ancient Greek mathematician **Archimedes** (c. 287–212 BC), whom Badiou is fond of citing in many contexts, did precisely this.

After his supposed discovery, Archimedes made a second statement, Badiou claims.

> ALTHOUGH THESE MATHEMATICAL TRUTHS ARE ETERNAL, THEY MUST APPEAR IN ORDER TO EXIST, TO BE EFFECTIVE IN THE WORLD.

This maxim underlies Badiou's ontology, since it says that for mathematical truth to exist an **event** must occur, it must somehow be presented from within the existing situation and lead to the point when it is indiscernible and the process of subjectivation can begin. In a procedure of this kind, the universal truth appears through a mathematical or scientific demonstration.

For the mathematical truth to exist it needs, as all truths, the process of subjectivation, it needs bodies and languages (brought together at the indiscernible point) for it to become part of an effective idea.

As we have seen, the example that Badiou provides in his *Logics of Worlds* for such a mathematical truth is the prime number.

The value of numbers

A prime number is an eternal mathematical truth. Since it is divisible only by prime numbers, that is, by the prime integer itself and the number 1, it transcends any set in which it may be, and thus any world in which it exists or inexists.

A prime number is a universal truth that is brought into being by the act of a mathematical operation, a demonstration in which a subject, faithful to it, uses it to construct a new mathematical situation (a generic set) …

... JUST AS THE TRUTH "HORSE" IS BROUGHT INTO BEING THROUGH AN ARTISTIC REPRESENTATION.

Beyond this, though, Badiou's primary thesis concerning the infinity of prime numbers is not simply their universality, but that the truth underlying them provides an important insight into the value of numbers generally – that they are all composed of the infinite, of prime numbers, or what he also calls their constituent atoms. *All non-prime numbers are composite numbers.*

THUS THE PHILOSOPHICAL CONDITION FOR SCIENCE AND MATHEMATICS IS THE EVENTAL TRACE OF THE PRIME NUMBER.

In defence of the universal and the infinite

As with the other truth procedures, we see here too Badiou's radical, emancipatory politics. Through this example Badiou is also defending his notions of universality, the concept of infinite truths, against democratic materialism and cultural relativism.

ADHERENTS TO THESE LATTER IDEOLOGIES SAY THAT SINCE MATHEMATICAL IDEAS ARE UNDERSTOOD DIFFERENTLY BY OTHER LANGUAGES, BODIES AND HISTORICAL CONTEXTS, THEN WHAT THEY REALLY REPRESENT ARE A REFLECTION OF THE CULTURE IN WHICH THEY ARE EXISTING.

In *Number and Numbers (Le Nombre et les nombres*, 1990) Badiou says that:

WE SEE HERE, AS IF IN THE PANGS OF ITS BIRTH, THE REAL ORIGIN OF THAT WHICH LYOTARD CALLS THE "LINGUISTIC TURN" IN WESTERN PHILOSOPHY, AND WHICH I CALL THE REIGN OF THE GREAT MODERN SOPHISTRY: IF IT IS TRUE THAT MATHEMATICS, THE HIGHEST EXPRESSION OF PURE THOUGHT, IN THE FINAL ANALYSIS CONSISTS OF NOTHING BUT SYNTACTICAL APPARATUSES, GRAMMARS OF SIGNS, THEN *A FORTIORI* ALL THOUGHT IS UNDER THE CONSTITUTIVE RULE OF LANGUAGE.

In turn, Badiou says that this in fact proves his own argument about the universality of such truths. If such mathematical ideas can appear and reappear in such widely disparate situations, then this suggests a **trans-temporality** to them and thus a non-finite, non-historical, real. (See the historical dimension of idea in the section below on communism, and the example of "horse" above.)

THEIR REAPPEARING, BECOMING CONSEQUENTIAL IN A DIFFERENT WORLD, IS PROOF OF THEIR UNIVERSALITY, IN SHORT, THEIR "PRIME-NESS".

The question of scientism

Related to his ethico-politics, Badiou is firmly against what he calls
scientism in philosophy, which says that the mind must be studied as
part of so-called nature, naturalized, and according to the scientific
protocols of neurology supported by a sublimated moralism.

THE PROBLEM WITH SCIENTISM IS THAT IT FAILS TO
RECOGNIZE THE IMMORTALITY OF SUBJECTS BY PLACING THE
FOCUS ON THE NATURALITY OF OBJECTS.

Also, moralism denies or does not know creative violence and radical
choice, only laws and orders, only ideology.

Badiou's ethics

Rather than reduce ethics to part of a pity for victims, Badiou proclaims that we should make ethics *the permanent maxim of singular procedures*, that is:

> INSTEAD OF MAKING ETHICS MERELY THE PROVINCE OF CONSERVATISM WITH A GOOD CONSCIENCE, IT SHOULD CONCERN THE DESTINY OF TRUTHS, IN THE PLURAL.

These statements from his book *Ethics: An Essay on the Understanding of Evil (L'éthique: Essai sur la conscience du Mal*, 1998) summarize well Badiou's theory of ethics, which is not only firmly grounded in and traceable throughout his philosophy, but firmly too in his radical leftist political position.

Badiou's ethics of truth is a dualist position in that the decision to make the ethical or unethical choice must be made, and that subsequently existence is the result of both ethical and unethical decisions.

WHAT IS ETHICAL IS THE FIRM COMMITMENT TO A SINGULAR TRUTH-EVENT – IN OTHER WORDS, THE FAITHFUL SUBJECT.

Any perversion of the truth by betrayal, delusion or the forced totalizing of it is the unethical, or "evil" (*le Mal*). Qualifying this position, let's go through briefly what he means by the unethical positions relative to a truth-event.

First and foremost for Badiou is the act of **betrayal**. This refers to the proverbial turning of the back by a subject on their fidelity to a truth when the consequences of a truth become hard and/or inconvenient for the person to maintain. This argument is valid for all of the categories of truth, the most obvious being love …

… BUT FOR BADIOU THIS IS ESPECIALLY THE CASE POLITICALLY IN WHAT HE CALLS THE **THERMIDORIAN ACT**, THE REJECTION BY A FAITHFUL SUBJECT OF THE REVOLUTION.

An unethical **delusion** is a fidelity to a false event, the confusion of a simulacrum of a truth-event with a real one, which instead of defending the truth of an event in fact reinforces the status quo. This runs contrary to Badiou's ethical position, to the whole philosophy of the event.

An unethical disaster is the attempt by a subject to **totalize** the truth to which they are faithful. That is, although it is ethical to stay faithful to a truth, it is unethical to force a *conversion of the unfaithful*, to force a nomination of the unnameable truth into a particular world of knowledge, i.e. the forcing of the subjectivity of the truth into the objectivity of knowledge.

A SIMPLE EXAMPLE WOULD BE THE TURNING OF THE TRUTH OF THE CHRIST EVENT INTO A RELIGIOUS PRACTICE OF DEFINITE, POSITIVE RULES AND LAWS THAT ATTEMPT TO TOTALIZE THE ACTIONS OF ALL BODIES AND MERGE TRUTHS INTO ONE TRUTH, INTO A WHOLE, UNCRITICAL CHRISTIAN LIFE.

Ethics and the act of thinking

Instead of turning the subjectivity of an unnameable truth into the basis for a single absolute epistemology, the *ethical subject remains faithful to the truth as an underlying idea that encourages constant thinking* – as opposed to, say, a repetition of religious, or any, principles/laws – and the acting of the subject according to generic truth, not a pre-determined knowledge-construction.

This type of ethics Badiou opposes to what he calls the "ideology of ethics", today's Western ethics, which is at its core bourgeois in that it encourages intervention by the defenders of the decided universal Good into the lives and affairs of others. The ideology of ethics is grounded in the humanist position, in the abstract notion that there are universal, general human rights and that the defender of the abstract Good (the great wealthy, Western benefactor and capitalist exploiter) has an ethical responsibility to protect the supposed victim, i.e. those excluded from Western ethics.

No general ethics, no universal rights

Badiou's ethics of truths operates in the opposite manner. Instead of being a defence of a particular established situation, it is the result of a truth-event, fidelity to the truth of a particular event, and thus for Badiou there can be no general ethics, no universal human rights; an ethical or unethical position is always determined according to a truth-event, to a particular way of thinking …

… A SUBTRACTION FROM, AND NOT ACTUALLY OF, A CERTAIN SITUATION.

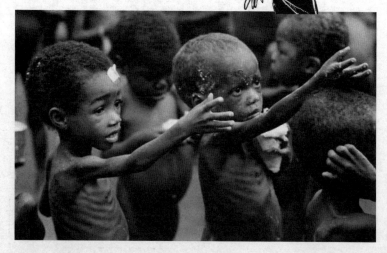

Since Badiou's ethics is based on fidelity to the truth-event it avoids the bourgeois implications of the totalizing ideology of ethics. It is not a result of the *consolidation of differences* around an abstract, universal Good (the non-thought of the power position), but the proximity to a *vulnerable site* within that situation where the event-break occurs.

A radical ethics

Badiou's ethics also challenges common understandings of fidelity and ethics in that it demands, for example, the abandoning of one's long-term partner for the chance occurrence of a newly found love.

YOU MUST RUN AFTER THE NEW LOVE, REMAIN FAITHFUL TO THAT PERSON AND TRUTH, AND NOT TO THE PERSON THAT IS STILL FAITHFUL TO THE OLD TRUTH.

The same is to be said of politics, science and art. This is a radical ethics in that it breaks with the drive for non-thinking, non-truth-conservancy, the "good" as it is commonly applied.

To give up on the present and run for the other is a dangerous ethics. To this Badiou would say that we must be keenly aware of what is a real truth-event and what is a false one.

It is our responsibility to choose and to be able to know the false from the real truth. Badiou's is a strong ethical burden to bear.

Circumstancing Badiou

Formally speaking, "political philosophy" is a disaster for Badiou, not to mention an oxymoron. There cannot be a merging of politics and philosophy in this way since doing so would destroy their respective autonomies: that of the evental power of the truth procedure politics, and that of philosophy to subsequently interrogate it. Nonetheless, Badiou's philosophy is fundamentally a political project.

ONE CANNOT SEPARATE MY PHILOSOPHY FROM MY POLITICS – THEY COMPLEMENT ONE ANOTHER – AND ONE WOULD BE MISTAKEN TO ATTEMPT TO DO SO.

LOSING ITS EDUCATION

Therefore it should be no surprise that a significant portion, if not all, of Badiou's work represents the circumstancing of his politics. Let's begin with the driving force of it all, Badiou's fidelity to the communist idea.

Shattering comforts and anomalies

Badiou says that a new truth is the most significant, the hardest, revolution humanity can face today because it demands a chance, the risk of shattering the existing situation with its negotiated **comforts** and accepted **anomalies**.

The communist idea

Communism is the idea of a society in which the *principle of equality* is the prevailing political truth and as such is a world that is not shaped by classical social relations. Communism is the idea that the world should not be governed by private property, but rather be one of equality and free association.

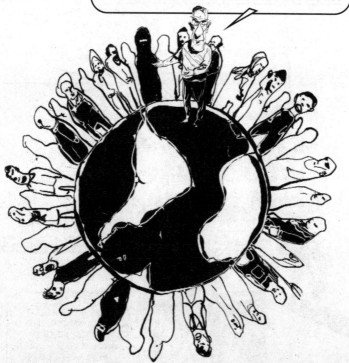

THIS UNIVERSAL, INFINITE IDEA OF COLLECTIVE LIFE MUST BE THE GUIDING TRUTH FOR ANY NEW POLITICAL WORLD, FOR ALL FUTURE FORMS OF POLITICAL EMANCIPATION WHATEVER THEIR NAME.

This is the essence of Badiou's whole *oeuvre*, the ethical position of fidelity to a universal idea – for him communism – that guides but does not force.

What, more precisely, does Badiou mean by the idea, and how does it relate to his vision of communism as a hypothesis for universal, political emancipation?

An idea for Badiou is the abstraction of its three fundamental elements: a *truth procedure*, a *belonging to history*, and an *individual subjectivation*. The operation of the idea of communism subsequently needs three basic elements: a political, a historical, and a subjective.

1. The **political element** of the idea is pretty straightforward.

2. Once the idea is possible after the event, then it finds its way into existence through a **historical inscription** within a type of truth (e.g. artistic, amorous, mathematical/scientific, or political), a process that includes an interaction of the idea with different types of truths at different points in human time.

3. Finally, there is the **subject** element needed for the operation of the idea of communism. This refers to the possibility for an individual, a human animal, to choose to become part of the new truth, to become faithful to it, a *militant* of it.

THAT IS, AN INDIVIDUAL BODY, WITH ALL ITS POTENTIALITIES, THOUGHTS, AFFECTS, ETC., BECOMES PART OF THE BODY-OF-TRUTH, THE MATERIAL EXISTENCE OF THE COMMUNIST IDEA, IN THE CONSTRUCTING OF A NEW REALITY, A NEW WORLD.

Beyond the individual

Thus, in the communist idea an individual goes beyond the limits of animality/individualism, of competition, selfishness, even finitude in becoming a militant for a new subjectivity. This choice represents, again, subjectivation, the process whereby an individual determines the place of a truth in their own life, in their existence.

The individual's decision to participate in a body-of-truth is a historical one, that is, thanks to the aforementioned process and abstraction of the idea, the individual in becoming part of the new subject recognizes his or her belonging to history.

IN COMMUNISM AS IT PLAYED OUT, THE COMMUNITY BECAME THE VERY COMING ITSELF OF THE COLLECTIVE AS TRUTH (THE IDEA INTO POLITICS).

Now, let's go back to the heart of the abstraction idea, the historical dimension. It is here that we encounter the complexity of history for the communist idea – and the core of Badiou's argument about the communist idea and its possibilities for political emancipation. There needs to be a trans-temporal availability of truths for an idea to be universal, for the communist idea to live again.

FROM THIS WE CAN SEE THAT THE IDEA OF COMMUNISM MUST NOT BE TIED TO ONE HISTORICAL SITUATION!

TRABAJO PERSONAL
RESPONSABILIDAD COLECTIVA

The 20th century, the Soviet experience, Cuba, the Kibbutz, etc. are examples of the appearing of the universal idea of community, representing possibilities for its being, but certainly not the only ones. To appreciate the universal we must, following the advice of Marxist theorist **Fredric Jameson** (b. 1934), *historicize*.

Finally, and not least of all, we must be extremely careful not to equate this sense of the communist idea as ideology to the totalizing one that Badiou considers the unethical.

THE COMMUNIST IDEA IS IDEOLOGICAL IN THE SENSE THAT IT IS AN OPERATION FOR THE FULL BECOMING OF A TRUTH AND ITS PRESERVATION AFTER THE COMPLETION OF ITS TRAJECTORY, THE PRESERVATION OF THE UNIVERSALITY OF THE TRUTH, THE GIVING TO THE COMMUNIST TRUTH OF POST-EVENTAL CONSEQUENCES.

Where is the communist idea today?

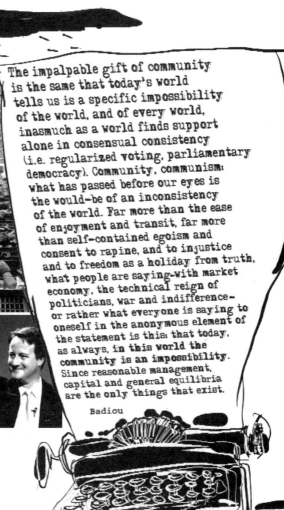

The impalpable gift of community is the same that today's world tells us is a specific impossibility of the world, and of every world, inasmuch as a world finds support alone in consensual consistency (i.e. regularized voting, parliamentary democracy). Community, communism: what has passed before our eyes is the would-be of an inconsistency of the world. Far more than the ease of enjoyment and transit, far more than self-contained egoism and consent to rapine, and to injustice and to freedom as a holiday from truth, what people are saying-with market economy, the technical reign of politicians, war and indifference- or rather what everyone is saying to oneself in the anonymous element of the statement is this: that today, as always, in this world the community is an impossibility. Since reasonable management, capital and general equilibria are the only things that exist.

Badiou

We can see here quite clearly an echoing of what Badiou says about today's negotiation of love through online dating websites, namely, the satisfying and encouraging of our narcissistic desire for risk-management, equilibrium, the avoidance of the event … let's stay put.

What Badiou is saying here is that today we believe only in what we can see; *that what exists must be what is reasonable.*

The inexistent of the world today (the non-logic of the universal idea of communism, its non-appearing) is thus the impossibility of community. To be *of the* world means to make the impossibility of the community, the real of communism, one's own impossibility; this is the singularized possibility of being-in-the-world.

The popular imperative of today is: manage all of your thoughts and actions in such a way that they attest to the impossibility of community, to act "in the absence of idea", to live without fidelity to an idea.

Terror and disaster

Okay, so what should radical leftists do? What is Badiou's theory of action? How can the idea of community come into being?

FORMALLY SPEAKING, WE MUST PRODUCE **TERROR**, WITHOUT WHICH THE NATURAL MOVEMENT OF THINGS LIES IN THE DISSIDENCE OF THE POWER OF THE RICH.

This should not be misconstrued with the popular, media and state rhetoric, or at all be seen as a blanket support for violence. This terror is a projection of a subjective maxim onto the state – in short, a desire for equality. Badiou says that we must state the nothingness of our situation, to think and say that this – the present – ought not be (the violent demand of the love-event). This thinking produces what Badiou terms "terror", but could just as easily be called shock, surprise or trauma.

In contrast to this is what Badiou terms "disaster".

The disaster is an important concept for Badiou's theory of action since it elicits the philosophical desire for negation and politics, and in so doing warns us again that *philosophy cannot produce a truth*: this can only be done through a truth procedure, e.g. politics, science, art or love.

Separating communism from politics

The only way we can remain faithful to the communist idea, to emancipatory politics regardless of its past historicizations, is to work hard to preserve terror and to avoid a disaster. We must separate the politics of emancipation from the acts and names of philosophy – the **de-suturing** of politics from philosophy – and in so doing avoid disaster by maintaining the need for terror, the event, the undecidable chance.

THUS, FOR COMMUNISM TO REAPPEAR IN THE WORLD WE MUST SEPARATE IT, DE-SUTURE IT, FROM THE POLITICAL.

In this way we protect the universality of the truth, of collective life, from the finitude of historicization, from the horrors of "really existing" communism of the 20th century.

This will allow us to go back to the *point* (the modality of the indiscernible) when the subject is born, to begin to trace the event and the decisions made regarding fidelity to it and the subsequent forcing of a future perfect. From there we can make alternative choices that will lead us to "fail again, fail better", as Marxist cultural critic **Slavoj Žižek** (b. 1949) reminds us.

For Badiou, the apparent failures of the communist hypotheses are not failures of the idea or the communist truth, but stages in the history of the communist hypothesis' becoming.

Badiou says that failures in the history of modern emancipatory politics, in the attempts at communism, have been to do with the poor decisions of subjects at moments within the trajectory of a truth.

The role of the philosopher

Once communism is again actual in the world, is finite and historical, the role of the philosopher will be to attack it, to criticize it constantly since s/he must, according to Badiou, always criticize the world as it is simply because it is as it is.

Also, once the communist idea re-emerges, this historicization of it will necessarily end because at some moment it will be confronted with the unnameable that will unravel its truth in the world and relegate it back to the real.

WE ARE THUS FACED WITH A PHILOSOPHICAL ARGUMENT THAT DEMANDS FIDELITY TO THE EVENT OF THE COMMUNIST IDEA DESPITE THE FACT THAT EVENTUALLY IT WILL FAIL.

This is the beauty of the argument, though: that we must keep striving to fail better, that existence is never an end, there is no place for eschatological (thinking the end of history, of time), theological or what Badiou calls religious thinking in this philosophy, or theory of history, nor is there for belief in a permanent stasis … the philosopher's work is never done, she must carry on in perpetuity.

Furthermore, even if all realities, all worlds are finite, there is no telling how long they will exist, which very well could seem like infinity when compared to human existence.

Finally on the communist idea, the reality of a world, indeed the world itself, changes when its subjects alter their relation to the impossible – the way the system of knowledge relates to the impossibility changes. So even though the impossibility is still impossible, the first step is to confront it, to challenge the prevailing opinion today that radical change is impossible.

Sarkozy: the man, the figure

In his writing on **Nicolas Sarkozy** (b. 1955) we see a clear example of Badiou's politics of emancipation. Badiou criticizes Sarkozy not simply as a politician of right-wing, anti-society, anti-community politics.

EVEN WORSE THAN SARKOZY THE PERSON IS SARKOZY THE FIGURE, WHAT HE REPRESENTS – THE DEATH OF THE LEFT IN FRANCE, IN THE WEST.

AND NOT ONLY THE DEATH OF THE LEFT BUT THE MOCKING OF ITS DEMISE BY THE RICH.

The aftermath of Sarkozy's May 2007 election to the presidency of France was not at all a surprise, Badiou says. It was in fact this lack of surprise, this confirmation of expectation that was most depressing for the left in France. There was no chance of any upset, no last-minute shock; any wager or risk seemed to have been eliminated.

The status quo of right-wing capitalism and parliamentarianism ruled the day unquestioned. The old left, even the old left-centre, had not only collapsed – it was so far removed from any significance that a person like Sarkozy, with his lavish and ostentatious galas, dinners and yachts could be elected.

The victory of Sarkozy demonstrated once again the manifest powerlessness of any sort of radical, leftist, emancipatory politics within the electoral system, set up to record preferences while excluding any truly dissenting political opinions.

Badiou on the barricades

WE MUST REMAIN CONTEMPORARIES OF MAY '68! WE MUST LIVE WITH AN IDEA, NOT UNDER THE EMPTY SLOGAN "GET RICH!"

Too many people today think that there is no alternative to a selfish, narcissistic life. We must have the courage to cut from these people, we must do something that is very simple, and that Plato said millennia ago: Live with an idea! Real politics begins only with such a conviction.

These are Badiou's sentiments, but what does he mean by fidelity to May '68?

Badiou is referring here to the radical truth-event (the fresh excitement of which appears in his fictional writings of the 1960s and 1970s) of spring and summer 1968 in Paris.

May 1968 was the culmination in France of the largest-ever general strike, of 11 million workers, sparked by student riots, protests, police brutality and collusion, and 400 committees for grievances against the right-wing government of President Charles de Gaulle.

ON 30 MAY, A CROWD OF NEARLY HALF A MILLION PEOPLE MARCHED THROUGH PARIS CHANTING "ADIEU, DE GAULLE!"

Nonetheless, all of the rioting was for nothing as de Gaulle's party was re-elected in late June with a massive majority, taking 353 of 486 parliamentary seats, while the socialists received 57 and the communists only 34. De Gaulle's election victory was not only overwhelming in and of itself, but relative to the situation and French political history. His majority was even stronger than before the events of May '68 and was the largest of the right since just after the First World War.

PEOPLE HAD TURNED THEIR BACKS ON THE "REVOLUTION" OR SIMPLY REACTED AGAINST IT OUT OF FEAR OF THE COLLAPSE OF THE SECURITY OF THE KNOWN.

EVEN THE COMMUNISTS HAD ONLY RELUCTANTLY SUPPORTED THE PROTESTORS WHOM THEY SAW AS ANARCHISTS.

"The red years"

Perhaps this is the reason why now, nearly 50 years later, Badiou advocates a non-state communism, a return to the communist idea of collective life but not the subjective decisions formerly made about it. This perceived infidelity and anti-revolutionary, anti-communist reaction by Badiou's friends, colleagues, people he admired and his fellow French *citoyens* more broadly, still fuels his thoughts and actions today, and in raw form, is the core of his entire philosophy.

This reaction against the events of May '68 had a profound effect on Badiou. Although already from 1960 he was committed to egalitarian ideals it was from May '68 to the 1980s, what Badiou refers to as "the red years", that he developed his political conviction to what can be termed communism and to which he is still a faithful subject. It is the period when he finally found, he says, harmony between his politics and love.

Badiou has called the experience of May '68 his "road to Damascus", a reference to the Biblical story of Saul's conversion to Christianity along the road to Damascus as he was travelling to persecute Christians. After this revelation Saul believed Christ to be the Messiah, the resurrected Christ as the event-trace of the true love event (again we see the close relation between love and politics) of the coming of the Messiah.

In line with this spirit of universality he made the choice to dislocate his name from the particularity of his Jewish identity, going from Saul to Paul.

Similarly for Badiou, May '68 was the event that revealed to him the truth of universality, of the idea of collective life called communism. One could argue that all of Badiou's philosophy and politics after the event of May '68 represent his fidelity to the trace of that truth-event. It is particularly the apostasy of Badiou's fellow '68ers, their Thermidorianism, their reversals of support for the spirit of the '68 event, that drive Badiou. He has never forgotten nor forgiven this betrayal.

AS WITH PAUL'S VISION OF SALVATION AND SUBSEQUENT CONVERSION, MY OWN SELF-CONFESSED SALVATION AND CONVERSION GAVE ME THE DRIVE TO PREACH THE NEW WORD, TO TEACH, WRITE, THINK AND VOCALIZE THE NEW, THE COMING REALITY.

Views of an event: variations on May '68

Badiou argues that there were four different May '68s, each with its own unique factors:

1. The most remembered was that it was primarily a student uprising, a revolt of the school and university students.

SUCH UPRISINGS WERE HAPPENING AROUND THE WORLD AT THAT TIME; THIS WAS NOT A FRENCH PHENOMENON ...

... AND SCHOOL AND UNIVERSITY STUDENTS REPRESENTED ONLY A TINY PERCENTAGE OF THE YOUNG, AND THEY WERE THE MIDDLE CLASS, WIDELY SEPARATED FROM THE WORKING-CLASS YOUNG.

Within this May '68 we see also adherence to Marxist language and to violence.

2. The second May '68 was that of the general strike of the workers, organized by factories and unions, a more classically "left" event. There are three unique and innovative aspects of this May '68. These strikes were largely launched and run by younger workers, and already had begun in 1967, and thus were not a result of May '68.

WHAT IS UNIQUE IS THAT WE SEE HERE A LINK BETWEEN A WORKERS' MOVEMENT AND THEN A STUDENT REVOLT.

Another radical aspect of this second May '68 was the systematic occupation of factories, which then had red flags flown at them. Finally, there was the kidnapping of factory bosses and minor battles with security.

3. The third May '68 Badiou refers to as the "libertarian May", the changing sexual and moral climate, and individual freedom, which gave rise to sexual freedom, gay rights and the women's movement, as well as new forms of theatre, political action and collective expression.

4. There is a fourth May '68, which Badiou says is the crucial one, still affecting the future very much, and this was not the immediate action of May '68 but the period of the ten years following, the "Mitterrand years".

THIS '68 DECADE WITNESSED THE END OF AN OLD STYLE OF POLITICS, LEADING TO A COLLECTIVE OBSESSION WITH THE QUESTION, "WHAT IS POLITICS?"

This was united under the same language in the belief of an objective historical actor, e.g. the working class; however, this language signified by the red flag was dying out.

Mao '69?

In Badiou's fidelity to communism we can see a close relationship with the thought of **Mao Tse-tung** (1893–1976).

Mao was the founder of the People's Republic of China and Chairman of its governing Communist Party from 1946 until his death in 1976. In his theoretical writings, revolutionary activities and actions as a leader of the Republic he defended Marxism and Leninism, worked closely with the Soviet Union and fought vigorously against capitalism/imperialism and all forms of social inequality both domestically and abroad … sometimes with exceptional brutality.

Badiou says that May '68 and its aftermath was the formative event of his metaphorical conversion, but some argue that the chief event of his thinking happened in 1969 when Badiou encountered, and became part of, the UCFML (*Union des communistes de France Marxiste-Léniniste*), the third-largest Maoist organization in France by 1970, and its publication *Le Marxiste-Léniniste*.

More than a decade later, in 1982, the same year that Badiou published *Theory of the Subject*, the UCFML published a statement on their views, saying that when some hear "Maoism" – that the UCFML is Maoist – they believe that the UCFML is marching with the Chinese.

IN REPLY, WE SAY THAT, IN CONTRAST TO OTHER GROUPS, WE DO NOT OWE ANYTHING TO CHINA AND ARE USING AND INTERPRETING MAO BASED ON OUR OWN EXPERIENCES IN FRANCE.

Such an approach to Mao certainly reflects Badiou's wider argument that it is from our own past and experiences that we must traverse through to reach beyond, since this is the site of the event and is where relevant truths derive, being as they are materialist creations.

Mao and egalitarianism

Badiou's interest in Mao is evident throughout his texts, but most obvious is their shared commitment to egalitarian principles. Mao's message during the Chinese Cultural Revolution was for communists not to let the Party become another bourgeois, a new bureaucracy, as was happening in the USSR. This warning against the monopoly of state power and its attempted elimination of radical difference and change is certainly in line with Badiou's thinking.

Any transition to communism, Mao states, requires a radical break from the existing situation, the ability to throw away the laws that exist and start anew, reconstitute the present based on the emancipatory principles of communism. In other words, without the truth-event of communism followed by subjective activism, the appearing and subjectivation of the communist idea via subjective fidelity to it, there can formally speaking be no transformation, no new reality guided by the communist idea. This brings us to another important Maoist concept for Badiou:

Badiou often repeats this axiom from Mao, using it as an allegory to describe various situations.

What Badiou means is that one can be both multiple and singular; the axiom is a way of representing the complexities of an ontology of event and of multiple singularity.

An example is the philosophical opposition between Badiou and a friend of over 50 years. Although both built their philosophies via a common reference to Sartre (as truth), their arguments are diametrically opposed, and thus it is proven that "one divides into two", that is, one epistemological world is split into two.

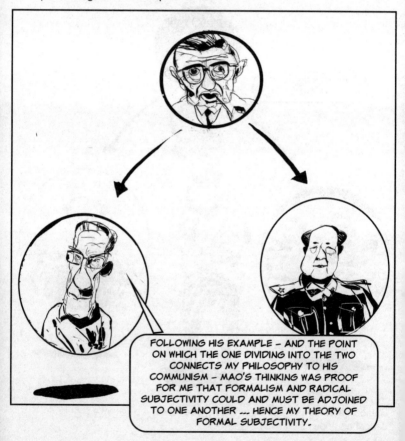

FOLLOWING HIS EXAMPLE – AND THE POINT ON WHICH THE ONE DIVIDING INTO THE TWO CONNECTS MY PHILOSOPHY TO HIS COMMUNISM – MAO'S THINKING WAS PROOF FOR ME THAT FORMALISM AND RADICAL SUBJECTIVITY COULD AND MUST BE ADJOINED TO ONE ANOTHER ... HENCE MY THEORY OF FORMAL SUBJECTIVITY.

Khmer Rouge: *"Je le regrette"*

In an article in *Le Monde* on 17 January 1979 Badiou openly declared his support for the Khmer Rouge communists, labelling the media attacks on them an anti-Cambodia campaign, and stating *"Kampuchea vaincra!"*, that is, "Kampuchea will overcome!" (referring to the Khmer Rouge-led state).

A communist, Badiou is an advocate of emancipation of the people against stronger, capitalist hegemonic (politically dominant) powers.

Sadly, the Khmer Rouge, it turned out, committed awful acts against the people of Cambodia, including arbitrary executions and genocide, social engineering programmes and failed agricultural reforms aimed at total self-sufficiency (a goal of many nations). Badiou's defence of the Khmer Rouge has thus in retrospect been roundly criticized.

In an interview published in *Le Point* on 14 May 2012 Badiou expressed his formal regret ("*Je le regrette*") for his enthusiasm in the 1970s over the victory of the Khmer Rouge. He was excited, he says, because it was an amazing victory of a small military, a small people, over the massive US military and its local allies.

THE VICTORY OF THE KHMER ROUGE WAS PROOF OF MAO'S STATEMENT THAT A WEAKER, POORER, SMALLER PEOPLE, IF UNITED, COULD DEFEAT A SUPERPOWER.

Badiou notes that his 1979 article was primarily against the politically motivated – not humanitarian or socially intended – invasion of Cambodia by the Vietnamese.

Badiou suggests that we can learn from his mistake in defending the Khmer Rouge.

This is why for Badiou one of the key tasks of contemporary politics, which seeks the emancipation of all humanity, is to redefine what it means to be victorious. We as supporters of emancipatory politics must be careful not to totalize radical activity, to totalize an idea.

"What does a Jew want?"

A rite of passage for leftists today often depends on their expressed opinion of the situation of Israel/Palestine. Despite his role in Udi Aloni's book, *What Does a Jew Want?: On Binationalism and Other Spectres* (2011), where he expresses his personal familial connections to the land and its people, Badiou does not write extensively on Israel/Palestine. This is perhaps because of former lessons about remaining cautious in presenting a zealous commitment to a radical cause that may not be a true event.

WHEN I SAY SOMETHING ON THE TOPIC, IN CONTRAST TO THE EMPTY TROPES AND UNINFORMED RHETORIC THAT IS THE MAINSTREAM DISCOURSE, I ENGAGE THE SUBJECT AT THE PRIMARY LEVEL OF THE CONCEPT OF "JEW".

Within the wider question of the political category of "other", Badiou asks what is the legitimate and appropriate political usage today of the category "Jew"?

In order for "Jew" to have any political, progressive significance, and for Jewish Israelis to be able to think something radically new – the impossible in the situation today – it must not continue to be defined by Israel according to negative external definitions, by those meanings simply turned ethically upside down.

If "Jew" is to mean something outside of negative external categories, there needs to be an open discussion on four main points:

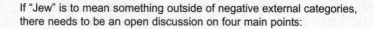

1. WHAT RELATION DOES "JEW" HAVE WITH ISRAEL AND ITS STATE POLICIES AND PRACTICES?

2. HOW IS "JEW" DEFINED BY JEWISH RELIGION?

3. WHAT IS THE ROLE OF THE MATRILINEAL CHARACTER OF JUDAISM – SINCE THE RETURN FROM BABYLON – WITH "JEW"? WHAT PLACE DOES RACE HAVE WITH DEFINING A "JEW"?

4. WHAT IS THE AFFILIATION OF "JEW" WITH THE REVOLUTIONARY ENGAGEMENT OF JEWS IN THE 1930S, 1940S AND SO ON?

Why raise these points? The aim is to criticize the use of the categories of "other" within cultural relativism – multiculturalism – in which categories represent the interests of a specific group within society.

> IF WE ARE TO BE FAITHFUL TO EGALITARIANISM AND EMANCIPATORY POLITICS, CATEGORIES OF OTHER SHOULD BE POLITICAL IN THE SENSE OF THE OTHER'S UNIVERSAL RELATIONSHIPS TO POWER .... TO THE STATE, RELIGION, HISTORY, RACE AND REVOLUTION.

The party and the state

On the abolition of state and political frontiers and the withering away of the state:

For Mao, Badiou maintains, the state must by definition be oppressive, either of internal or external forces. This is its nature, it can't be any other way – it fights for its own survival. Even if there are no more internal enemies, that is, if the state is in a situation of emancipatory politics, of communism, if imperialism still exists in the world outside of that state, then the communist state will only mean arrests, prisons, armies, executions, etc.

The Cultural Revolution in China showed us the limits of Leninism, and that any politics of emancipation cannot work under the old paradigm of revolution and party-state; for a state, revolution is nothing but an intervening period. This is why, again, the answer to fighting capitalism today is not the building of a communist state, but making the communist **idea** appear as a guiding truth that transcends the present state of states.

For true emancipation we must think beyond the state paradigm. We see this maxim throughout Badiou's texts, including in discussions about "actually-existing" communism. In reference to Cuba's honourable perseverance and political resistance against the US imperial capitalist model, he says it is doomed to failure because of its outmoded commitment to the figure of the party-state, which belongs to another era.

IT IS ETHICAL THAT CUBA REMAINS FAITHFUL TO COMMUNISM AS UNIVERSAL TRUTH, BUT A NEW POLITICAL EVENT AND TRUTH VIS-A-VIS THE PARTY-STATE MODEL NEEDS TO EMERGE FOR COMMUNISM TO LIVE TODAY.

Democracy: a "weak negation"

PARLIAMENTARY DEMOCRACY IS THE AUTHORIZED REPRESENTATIVE OF CAPITAL!

Karl Marx (1818–83)

… a conclusion that Badiou agrees with and uses to describe his own stance against the party-state system. Badiou calls democracy a "weak negation", an act so far removed from the destructive negation of Marxism that it is improper to call it anything other than what **Jürgen Habermas** (critical theorist and pragmatic philosopher, b. 1929) refers to as "consensus". This is because in order to participate in the democratic system you must be subject to it, you must conform to the subjectivity that it requires, to "the principle of 'this is the way it is, there's nothing to be done', the principle of Maastricht, of a Europe in conformity with the financial markets", according to Badiou.

We already know this quite well, since leftist after leftist party elected to office disappoints us, breaks promises, and this is not – it should not be seen as – a matter of any party's or person's corruption but as a result of the form of the system in which they operate. People who are elected don't as a rule change their minds, or their personal beliefs, but their subjectivity to the parliamentary system demands that they act accordingly, or be expelled.

THE PARLIAMENTARY SYSTEM IS FAITHFUL TO CAPITALISM AND THE MARKET FORCES IT REPRESENTS AND CONTROLS, AND THIS IS THE FIDELITY TO WHICH MEMBERS OF THE STATE MUST ADHERE, REGARDLESS OF WHAT THEY SAID BEFORE ENTERING THE SYSTEM.

There is no way out of this except **not** to be a part of the parliamentary system, of the democratic process and its subsequent government.

One could argue that if the parliamentary democratic subjectivity was changed to one of reaction against capitalism then one could use the state-party system to alter the relationship to capital.

To effect real change we need not to vote or run for office but to create **the (truth) conditions** that will make the event appear and force those within the system to make alternative choices.

Global radical events

As a side-effect of the rise of the capitalist global market, potential sites of radical events are connected in ways like never before – an expansion and self-destructive tendency of capitalism foreseen by Marx – and perhaps we are starting to see for the first time the actual conditions necessary for a true Communist International that is neither state-controlled nor bureaucratic?

Whether or not this is the case, these new forms of global connection (though we need to be vigilant of the state's manipulation of these platforms) and recent radical, revolutionary events – the riots and revolts in places such as Brazil, Egypt, Mexico, Syria, Tunisia and Turkey, and the technologies such as mobile phones and social media potentially used to organize them – are providing increasing confidence that a political truth can be created without parliamentarianism and can be kept distant from the state ...

A revolutionary vs. a state revolutionary

A revolutionary is one who tries to force a new, alternative reality through fidelity to an event trace, who smashes the old truth and the consequences of fidelity to it (the present political situation). The state revolutionary on the other hand is a trans-worldly subject.

THE STATE REVOLUTIONARY TRIES TO SEPARATE STATE POLITICS FROM REVOLUTIONARY POLITICS ... WHILE WORKING WITHIN STATE POWER!

S/he tries to maintain the vitality of the lived consequences of a former truth – that is, the present reality – while adapting their functionality according to a new truth. S/he tries to accommodate the event to the existing structure. Thus, the state revolutionary does not go all the way in their fidelity to the new truth. Theirs is an unethical position doomed to failure.

Green is the new red, but really green

Being "green" today is commonly associated with liberalism, which is to say some sort of perceived "leftism". To be green is to "care", to care about the "environment" and by implication for life generally. Not to be green is not to love life, not respect the world around us; it is, so perceived, the right-wing, conservative position. For those who believe this dichotomy, Badiou says you need to wake up!

How can this be so? Because, Badiou argues, instead of breaking the system of capital, environmentalism provides it with brand-new avenues of investment, speculations and projects. Every proposition that, like environmentalism, immediately concerns the economy can be – and is by definition – assimilated to capital.

The novel philosopher

"Sartre and I are the last two eighteenth-century philosophers!" By this Badiou means that he and Sartre, in addition to a lifelong fidelity to consistent, active engagements in politics, are the last two French thinkers to present their philosophies in both the abstract form of philosophical treatises and through the more readily available, "living" characters of plays and novels.

MY FICTIONS, MY "ROMANOPÉRAS" (OR NOVEL-OPERAS), INCLUDING FOUR COMEDIES AND TWO TRAGEDIES, ARE MEANT AS ENTERTAINING EXPOSITIONS OF MY POLITICS AND ETHICS, AND OF MY PHILOSOPHY OF THE EVENT MORE GENERALLY.

Three of these demonstrate well not only Badiou's Sartrean circumstancing of philosophy into literature, but the subtle shifts in his political philosophy over several decades.

From 1972 to 1978 Badiou wrote the romanopéra *The Red Scarf* (*L'Echarpe rouge*). The structure of the play imitates that of *The Satin Slipper (Le Soulier de Satin)* by **Paul Claudel** (1868–1955). In the play, the local community party leadership in the north-east part of the play's fictional country calls for a general strike and launches a limited civil insurrection. This action fails, and following the failure the revolutionary organizations meet and discuss what to do next; their plan is direct military action emerging from the south of the country …

THE ESSENCE OF THE PLAY IS TELLING THE STORY OF A VICTORIOUS REVOLUTIONARY EVENT, AND MOST IMPORTANTLY OF THIS STORY BEING LEFT OPEN.

The Incident at Antioch (L'Incident d'Antioche), written 1982–89, was also inspired by a work of Paul Claudel, this time *The Town (La Ville)*. It is another fine example of a fictional manifestation of the becoming-subject within a new situation. In it, Badiou wants to reiterate the importance of universality to a new language of truth today – hence the characters of Céphas (St Peter) and Paule (a female St Paul), and Paule's conversion in Antioch.

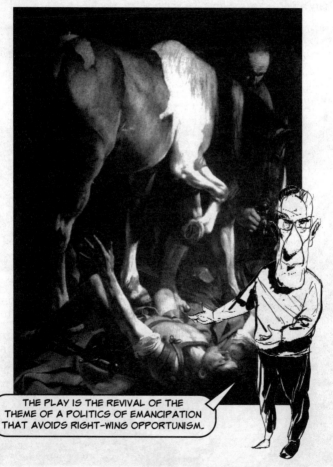

THE PLAY IS THE REVIVAL OF THE THEME OF A POLITICS OF EMANCIPATION THAT AVOIDS RIGHT-WING OPPORTUNISM.

Constant questioning of reality

In *The Incident at Antioch* there is a shocking revolution, whose leaders renounce the power that comes from victory. Céphas, the leader of the revolution, refuses to hold a post because his passion is in destruction, not construction; he is bored with rebuilding the state. Céphas represents the very purpose, the ethos, of philosophy for Badiou, not just for his non-dogmatic fidelity to a truth, but in the related act of constant questioning of reality not because of anything in particular but because it is as such.

WE ALSO SEE IN THIS TEXT THE CENTRAL ARGUMENT AGAINST THE STATE: THAT BY ITS FORM, A CONSTRUCTION OF IDEOLOGY AND NOT TRUTH, IT CANNOT BE ETHICAL.

The Incident at Antioch is then also an exposition of Badiou's ethics, of the ethical battle between truth and ideology, the ethics of fidelity to a truth versus the dogmatic adherence to an interpretation of it. The important difference between *The Red Scarf* and *The Incident at Antioch* is the optimism of the former and the sense of lost chances of the latter, written within a period of ending, the collapse of the revolutionary decades leading into the 1980s, and the popular closing off of their truths.

In his fiction of the 1990s, notably the several works dealing with the character Ahmed, Badiou works through the philosophical truth love, in particular showing how different interpretations, different movements around a truth, enhance the universality of that truth. The universal must remain open, its differences and potentialities must remain so; otherwise we are forever trapped in the present, in the finite. In a sense we see not a renewal *per se* of the optimism of the 1970s texts, but a reinvigorated spirit and hoped-for communism, wrapped around a fierce call for the universal, for the reintroduction of truth to European thought. The "later Badiou" was born.

To date, Badiou's non-philosophical works have rarely been read and almost never discussed by those without a fluent knowledge of French. This is likely to change rapidly over the next few years with the coming publication of his plays in English. Perhaps there'll even be the first performance of Badiou in English?

The rebirth of history

In a very late response to May '68, Badiou tries in *The Rebirth of History* (*Le Réveil de l'histoire*, 2011) to deal with the past failure of the revolts to effect lasting change – and in fact to lead to a counter-revolution by laying out his plan for a successful emancipatory movement structured around the operation of the communist idea.

What exactly is Badiou professing here by this call to overlook history for the sake of collective life and the reintroduction of thinking, of philosophy?

As we know already, the event is a break, a rupture of the continuum, a moving of being from the void. This redirects the course of history, since history is created by **dialectics** and by discourse.

More specifically, forgetting history means, Badiou says, to "make decisions of thought", to choose how to decide, to interpret, without reaching backwards and projecting forward our decisions of thought through the pre-existing or supposed historical chain of meaning.

To forget history is to think again at a point that is prior to a known chain of signifiers (the results of past communist attempts) in order to make a choice – an original, alternative one – on what we will do with that truth.

Forgetting history is to open the door to a different future, and it is to write an emancipatory politics that chooses its own axioms for drawing conclusions. Once this emancipatory idea has made such an "immanent determination", only then can it look to history.

Select Bibliography of Alain Badiou

1960s

Almagestes (Paris: Éditions du Seuil, 1964)
Portulans (Paris: Éditions du Seuil, 1967)
"Infinitesimal Subversion", *Le Marxiste-Léniniste*, 1968
"Mark and Lack: On Zero", *Le Marxiste-Léniniste*, 1969
Le Concept de modèle (Paris: François Maspéro, 1969), trans. Luke Fraser
& Tzuchien Tho, *The Concept of Model: An Introduction to the Materialist
Epistemology of Mathematics* (re. press, 2007)

1970s

Théorie de la contradiction (Paris: François Maspéro, 1975)
De l'idéologie (w. F. Balmès) (Paris: François Maspéro, 1976)
Le Noyau rationnel de la dialectique hégélienne (w. L. Mossot & J. Bellassen)
   (Paris: François Maspéro, 1977).
L'Écharpe rouge: Roman Opéra (Paris: François Maspéro, 1979)

1980s

Théorie du Sujet (Paris: Editions du Seuil, 1982), trans. Bruno Bosteels,
Theory of the Subject (New York: Continuum, 2009)
"Custos, quid noctis?", *Critique* 480 (1984)
Peut-on penser la politique? (Paris: Editions du Seuil, 1985)
"L'Usine comme site événementiel", *Le Perroquet*, No. 62–3 (22 April–10 May
1986), "The Factory as Event Site", trans. Alberto Toscano,
www.prelomkolektiv.org
L'Être et l'événement (Paris: Editions du Seuil, 1988), trans. Oliver Feltham,
Being and Event (London: Continuum, 2005)
Manifeste pour la philosophie (Paris: Editions du Seuil, 1989), trans. Norman
Madarasz, *Manifesto for Philosophy* (SUNY, 1999)
L'Incident d'Antioche: tragédie en trois actes, trans. Susan Spitzer, *The
Incident at Antioch: a Tragedy in Three Acts* (written in the 1980s, published
by Columbia Press, 2013)

1990s

Rhapsodie pour le théâtre (Paris: Imprimerie nationale, 1990)
Le Nombre et les nombres (Paris: Editions du Seuil, 1990), trans. Robin
Mackay, *Number and Numbers* (Malden, MA: Polity Press, 2008)
D'un désastre obscur (L'Aubre: La Tour d'Aigues, 1991)
Conditions (Paris: Editions du Seuil, 1992), trans. Steven Corcoran,
Conditions (London: Continuum, 2008)
L'Éthique (Paris: Hatier, 1993), trans. Peter Hallward, *Ethics: An Essay on the
Understanding of Evil* (New York: Verso, 2004)

Ahmed le subtil (Arles: Actes Sud, 1994)

Ahmed philosophie, suivi de Ahmed se fâche, théâtre (Arles: Actes Sud, 1995)

Beckett, l'increvable désir (Paris: Hachette, 1995), *On Beckett*, ed. N Power & A. Toscano (Manchester: Clinamen Press, 2003)

Les Citrouilles, comédie (Arles: Actes Sud, 1996)

Deleuze (Paris: Hachette, 1997), trans. Louise Burchill, *Deleuze: The Clamour of Being (Theory Out of Bounds)* (Minnesota Press, 1999)

Saint-Paul, la fondation de l'universalisme (Paris: Editions du Seuil, 1997), trans. Ray Brassier, *Saint Paul: The Foundation of Universalism* (Stanford, 2003)

Calme bloc ici-bas (Paris: P.O.L., 1997)

Court traité d'ontologie transitoire (Paris: Editions du Seuil, 1998)

Petit manuel d'inesthétique (Paris: Editions du Seuil, 1998), trans. Alberto Toscano, *Handbook of Inaesthetics* (Stanford Press, 2004)

Abrégé de métapolitique (Paris: Editions du Seuil, 1998), trans. Jason Barker, *Metapolitics* (New York: Verso, 2005)

2000s

Circonstances 1, Kosovo, 11 Septembre, Chirac/Le Pen (Paris: Leo Scheer, 2003)

Circonstances 2, Irak, foulard, Allemagne/France (Paris: Leo Scheer, 2004)

Circonstances 3, Portées du mot "juif" (Paris: Lignes, 2005)

Le Siècle (Paris: Editions du Seuil, 2005), trans. Alberto Toscano, *The Century* (Malden, MA: Polity, 2007)

L'Être et l'événement: Tome 2, Logiques des mondes (Paris: Editions du Seuil, 2006), trans. A. Toscano, *Being and Event II: Logics of Worlds* (London: Continuum, 2009)

Circonstances 4, De quoi Sarkozy est-il le nom? (Paris: Lignes, 2007)

"The Communist Hypothesis", *New Left Review* 49, January–February 2008, 29–42; *The Communist Hypothesis*, trans. David Macey & Steve Corcoran (New York: Verso, 2010)

Petit Panthéon portative (Paris: La Fabrique, 2008)

L'antiphilosophie de Wittgenstein (Caen: Editions Nous, 2009), trans. & intro. Bruno Bosteels, *Wittgenstein's Anti-Philosophy* (New York: Verso, 2011)

w. Nicolas Truong, *Éloge de l'amour* (Paris: Flammarion SA, 2009), trans. Peter Bush, *In Praise of Love* (London: Serpent's Tail, 2012)

Second manifeste pour la philosophie (Fayard, 2009), trans. Louise Burchill, *Second Manifesto for Philosophy* (Malden, MA: Polity Press, 2011)

Le fini et l'infini (Paris: Bayard, 2010)

Le Réveil de l'histoire (Nouvelles Editions Lignes, 2011), trans. Gregory Elliott, *Rebirth of History* (NY: Verso, 2012)

L'aventure de la philosophie française: Depuis le années 1960 (Paris: La Fabrique Editions, 2012), trans. Bruno Bosteels, *The Adventure of French*

Philosophy (London: Verso, 2012)
Mathematics of the Transcendental: Onto-logy of Being-There (London: Bloomsbury, 2013), trans. A.J. Bartlett & Alex Ling, but never published other than in English
"Affirmative Dialectics", *International Journal of Badiou Studies*, Vol. 2 (June 2013)

Some helpful sources on Badiou (all approved by Badiou)

Journal
Badiou Studies – www.badioustudies.org – published by Punctum Books

Books
Jean-Louis Krivine, *Théorie des ensembles* (Paris: Cassini, 1998)
Justin Clemens & Oliver Feltham, *Infinite Thought* (London: Continuum, 2003)
Sam Gillespie, *The Mathematics of Novelty: Badiou's Minimalist Metaphysics* (Melbourne: re. press, 2008)
Peter Hallward, *Think Again: Alain Badiou and the Future of Philosophy* (London: Continuum, 2004)
Ray Brassier & Alberto Toscano, *Theoretical Writings* (London: Continuum, 2004), which Badiou says is the best introduction to his work in English
Ed Pluth, *Philosophy of the New* (Malden, MA: Polity Press, 2010)
Bruno Bosteels, *Badiou and Politics* (Durham, NC: Duke Press, 2011)
François Laruelle, trans. Robin Mackay, *Anti-Badiou: the Introduction of Maoism into Philosophy* (London: Bloomsbury Publishing, 2013)

Also ...
The European Graduate School is continually posting lectures by Alain Badiou on their website at: www.egs.edu

Citations
Quotes have been taken from the following Badiou publications, with permission:

"Philosophy as Biography", *Lacanian Ink*, p. 30
Logics of Worlds, pp. 13, 25, 548, 594 © Alain Badiou, translated by Alberto Toscano 2009, *Logics of Worlds: Being and Event II*, Bloomsbury Academic, an imprint of Bloomsbury Publishing Plc
Conditions, pp. 124, 149; © Alain Badiou, translated by Steve Corcoran, 2008, *Conditions*, Continuum, by permission of Bloomsbury Publishing Plc
Ethics, pp. 3, 100, 120
In Praise of Love, p. 48; Badiou, Alain & Truong, Nicolas, *In Praise of Love*

(Serpent's Tail, London, 2012)

Number and Numbers, p. 58; © Polity Press, Cambridge UK, 2008 (translated by Robin Mackay from *Le Nombre et les Nombres* © Editions du Seuil, Paris, 1990)

Interview by Spitzer and Blanton, in *Incident at Antioch*, p. 140; by permission of Columbia University Press

Author's acknowledgements

I would like to thank some of the people who have contributed, in complementary ways, to the "eventing" of this book: Duncan Heath for his editing and publishing efforts, constant support and patience. Piero for his outstanding artwork. Arthur Rose for the long conversations on Badiou. Rolando Morales, Dwayne Dahlbeck, Jason Bruno, Andrew Erickson and Will Sturkey for their eternal friendship. Cheryl Ann Kelly, Stephanie Michelle Kelly and Lior Libman for their amazing love, strength and support. And last, but not least, Professor Alain Badiou, for the times he sat and chatted with me, and in general for his boundless generosity.

I dedicate this book to the memory of my father, Terrence Edward Kelly. A father, a husband, a brother, a friend, and a human being with faults and fears like the rest of us. I learn from his wisdom as much as from his mistakes. I will never forget his firm commitment to egalitarian principles, his belief in universal truth and his pedagogy of love above all else … not to mention his freakish basketball skills, inventor of the famed "Kelly shot".

Artist's acknowledgements

I would like to thank Duncan Heath for his trust and patience. I dedicate this book to my father, my sisters Rosana and Carolina Pierini and my mother who supports me blindly, also to all the Cruz family, my family and to the person I love the most.

Author biography

Michael J. Kelly is Visiting Professor at The Hebrew University of Jerusalem, and Library Fellow at The Van Leer Jerusalem Institute. His research intersects contemporary philosophical thought with critical theories of historiography and philosophy of history. He is the author of *Introducing Alain Badiou: A Graphic Guide* (London: Icon Books, 2014), *Speculative Objectivism: A Radical Philosophy of History* (New York: Punctum Books, forthcoming 2015), and several articles, reports and dialogues. He is, with Arthur J. Rose, co-General Editor of the journal *Badiou Studies* and co-convenor of *Lacan Read(s) Across the Disciplines*. He is also co-General Director and Editor of *Networks and Neighbours*, and General Director of the international seminar series, *Philosophies of History*.

Artist's biography

Piero is an illustrator, animator and graphic designer based in London since 1997. He is from La Plata (Argentina). His books in Icon Books' *Introducing* series include *Introducing Shakespeare, Introducing Anthropology, Introducing Psychiatry, Introducing Nietzsche, Introducing Barthes, Introducing Aesthetics*, and *Introducing Slavoj Žižek*.

Index

Ptolemy 8